SING and PLAY ANIMALS

PIE CORBETT

CHRYSALIS EDUCATION

FARM ANIMALS

SEE ALL THE ANIMALS

See all the animals on the farm,
Eee-eye, eee-eye, oh!
The big brown cow and her little calf,
Eee-eye, eee-eye, oh!
With a milk milk here,
And a milk milk there,
Here a milk, there a milk,
Everywhere a milk milk.
See all the animals on the farm,
Eee-eye, eee-eye, oh.

See all the animals on the farm,
Eee-eye, eee-eye, oh!
The mother sheep and her baby lamb,
Eee-eye, eee-eye, oh!
With a chew grass here,
And a chew grass there
Here a chew, there a chew,
Everywhere a chew chew.
See all the animals on the farm,
Eee-eye, eee-eye, oh.

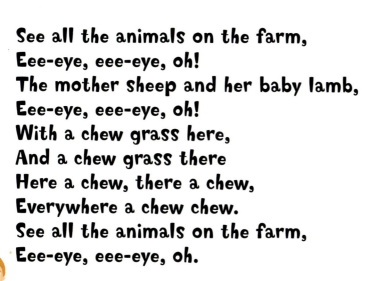

FARM ANIMALS

THINGS TO TALK ABOUT

Look at these farm animals.

Do you know their names?

What sounds do they make?

Can you match the mothers with their babies?

Have you ever visited a farm?

FARM ANIMALS

THE FARMER'S IN THE DEN

Sing and do the actions for this fun game!

The farmer's in his den,
The farmer's in his den,
Eee, eye, adyio,
The farmer's in his den.

The farmer takes a wife,
The farmer takes a wife,
Eee, eye, adyio,
The farmer takes a wife.

The wife takes a child,
The wife takes a child,
Eee, eye, adyio,
The wife takes a child.

The child takes a dog,
The child takes a dog,
Eee, eye, adyio,
The child takes a dog.

We all pat the dog,
We all pat the dog,
Eee, eye, adyio,
We all pat the dog.

GOOD MORNING MRS. HEN

Chuck, chuck, chuck,
Good morning Mrs. Hen.
How many chickens
have you got?

Madam, I've got ten.
Three of them are yellow,
And three of them are brown,
And four of them are
black-and-white,
The nicest in the town.

GOOD MORNING MRS. DUCK

Cluck, cluck, cluck,
Good morning Mrs. Duck.
How many ducklings have you got?
Madam, I've got ten.
Three of them are yellow,
And three of them are brown,
And four of them are speckled-red,
The nicest in the town.

Quack, quack, quack,
Good morning Mrs. Goose.
How many goslings have you got?
Madam, I've got ten.
Three of them are yellow,
And three of them are brown,
And four of them are grey-and-white,
The nicest in the town.

BIRDS

THINGS TO TALK ABOUT

1.

Look at these pictures.

What does picture 1 show?

What's happening in picture 2?

In picture 3, what are the babies doing?

Have you ever seen a nest?

2.

3.

THINGS TO DO

Make a delicious egg sandwich!

You need

butter   bread   fork   boiled egg   bowl   mayonnaise

1. Spread some butter on two slices of bread.

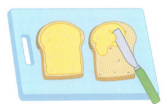

2. Using a fork, mash a boiled egg in a bowl.

3. Add a little mayonnaise, if you like.

4. Spread the egg mixture onto a slice of bread.

5. Cover with the other slice. It's ready to eat! Yummy!

PETS

MARY HAD A LITTLE LAMB

Mary had a little lamb,
Its fleece was white as snow,
And everywhere that Mary went
The lamb was sure to go.

It followed her to school one day,
That was against the rule,
It made the children laugh and play,
To see a lamb at school.

BILLY HAD A LITTLE DOG

Billy had a little dog,
It barked all night and day,
But when he went to calm it down,
The dog just liked to play.

Sandy had a little cat,
It slept all afternoon,
But every night the cat went out,
To prowl under the moon.

Naseem had a little fish,
It swam around its bowl,
It tried to leap into the air,
It was a happy soul!

PETS

THINGS TO TALK ABOUT

Look at Sam's pet hamster.

Where does it sleep?

What does it eat and drink?

How does it exercise?

Do you have a pet?

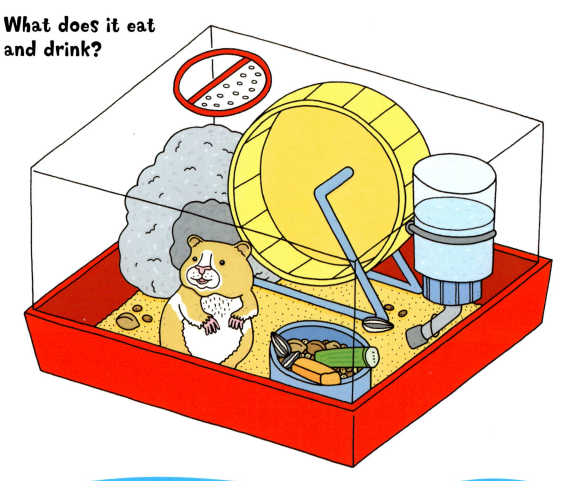

THINGS TO DO

Make your own pet mouse!

You need

two circles of card • ball of wool and piece of pink wool • scissors • black and pink felt • glue

1. Put the two card circles together and wind wool around them until you have filled up the hole with wool!

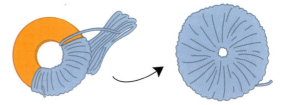

2. Ask an adult to cut between the two edges of the card circles.

3. Tie the piece of pink wool between the card circles, leaving a length for the tail. Now remove the card.

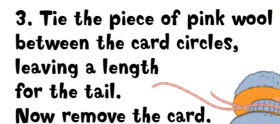

4. Cut out eyes, nose and ears from the felt. Stick them onto your pet mouse!

Scissors are sharp! Make sure an adult helps you.

ONE, TWO, THREE, FOUR, FIVE

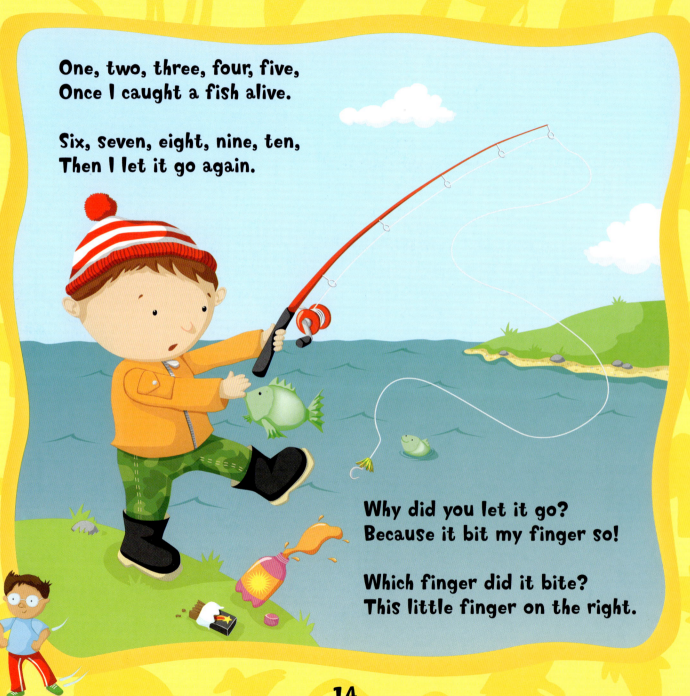

One, two, three, four, five,
Once I caught a fish alive.

Six, seven, eight, nine, ten,
Then I let it go again.

Why did you let it go?
Because it bit my finger so!

Which finger did it bite?
This little finger on the right.

FIVE LITTLE DOLPHINS

One, two, three, four, five,
Five little dolphins took a dive.
Six, seven, eight, nine, ten,
They splashed into the sea again!

Then where did they head?
Down through the waves to the smooth seabed.
What did they do down there?
Swam through the sea without a care!

One, two, three, four, five,
Five blue whales went for a dive.
Six, seven, eight, nine, ten,
Sleek and sure, they dived again!

Then where did they go?
Where the deepest waters flow.
What did they have to eat?
Fish and crabs, oh what a feast!

FISH

THINGS TO TALK ABOUT

Describe one of the fish you see here.

Ask your friends to guess which one you are looking at.

THINGS TO DO

Print a glittering fish!

You need

pencil   paper   paints   dish   rolled card   glitter

1. Draw an outline of a fish.

2. Dot on the fish's eye, with paint.

3. Pour paint into a dish and dip the rolled card into it.

4. Use this to print scales in 'c' shapes across the fish's body.

5. Before the paint fully dries, sprinkle on glitter to make the scales look shiny and wet!

WILD ANIMALS

OLD NOAH'S ARK

Old Noah once he built an ark,
And patched it up with hickory bark.
He anchored it to a great big rock,
And then began to load his stock.

The animals went in one by one,
The elephant chewing a carroway bun.

The animals went in two by two,
The crocodile and the kangaroo.

The animals went in three by three,
The tall giraffe and the tiny flea.

The animals went in four by four,
The hippopotamus got stuck in the door.

The animals went in five by five,
The bees mistook the bear for a hive.

The animals went in six by six,
The monkey was up to his usual tricks.

WILD ANIMALS

THE JUNGLE

The jungle is the place to be,
If animals you want to see.
Watch them as they pass on through,
But do look out — they might get you!

The snakes slither by, all in a queue,
The python hissed at the cock-a-too.
sssssssss!

The monkeys swing by, playing around,
The daddy gorilla slept on the ground.
zzzzzzzzzzz!

The tiger pads through, with long, sharp claws,
The leopard yawned his big, wide jaws.
yyyaaaaaawwn!

The insects fly by, all in a mass,
The bees buzzed round the hippopotamus.
buzzzzzzzzzzz!

WILD ANIVIALS

THINGS TO TALK ABOUT

Look at these wild animals.

Do you know their names?

Which have stripes and which have spots?

Which of these animals can be fierce?

Have you ever seen any wild animals?

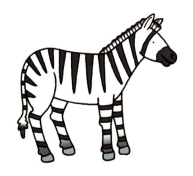

WILD ANIMALS

THINGS TO DO

Make a fun animal mask!

You need

pencil   card   scissors   paints   glue   pipe cleaners   popsicle stick

1. Draw an animal's face on to the card and ask an adult to cut it out for you.

2. Paint it in bright colors.

3. Attach some pipe cleaners for whiskers.

4. Glue the popsicle stick to the back of the mask for you to hold.

5. Now you have a wild animal mask to play with!

Scissors are sharp! Make sure an adult helps you.

RHYME ACTIONS

Why not add some actions to the rhymes to make them fun?
Here are a few to get you started, but you could make up your own too!

marching

turning around

going to sleep

reaching high

waving side to side

flying a plane

rocking a baby

touching the floor

dancing

stepping side to side

talking on the phone

stretching wide

HOW THE BOOK WORKS

The book is divided into five units: farm animals, birds, pets, fish, and wild animals.
Each unit comprises four pages.

 The first page of each unit features a well-known nursery rhyme or traditional rhyme.

 On the second page of the unit, the words to the rhyme have been changed so that children can sing about a topic, learning basic information in an enjoyable way.

 The third page of the unit provides a topic for discussion where children can draw on their own experience and broaden their knowledge.

 The fourth page offers an activity for really involving the children.

TEACHERS' AND PARENTS' NOTES

Where you see an "open book" icon in the bottom right corner of a page, this indicates that there are further ideas, suggestions, or an explanation about the page's contents.

Page 2 The rhyme should be repeated for all the other animals in the farmyard. Practice the animals' sounds with the children before singing.

Page 5 To play this game, the children stand in a circle and hold hands. One child is chosen to be the farmer and stands in the middle. They sing the first verse, skipping around the farmer in a circle. The children stand still, then the farmer chooses a wife to stand with him in the center of the circle. They sing the second verse, skipping around as before. The game continues like this until the final verse when the children all gather around the dog to gently pat him!

Page 7 Use this rhyme to practice basic counting and addition. Make a template of a chick and ask the children to draw around it to make the correct number of chicks for the duck or the goose. Next, they should color them and use them for basic addition exercises or for sorting into color sets.

Page 16 Lead a discussion about the different types of fish. If you can, visit an aquarium or spend some time looking at books in the library to see if the children can identify any of the fish. This activity could be used to introduce the concept of animal markings and why they are important.

Index

Animal sounds	2-3, 6-7, 19
Eating	9
Eggs	8-9
Farmer	2, 5
Hamster	12
Jungle	19
Mask	21
Milk	3
Mother animals	3-4, 6-8
Pets	11-13
Playing a game	5
Scales	17
Spots	20
Stripes	20

This U.S. edition copyright © 2006 Chrysalis Education
Published in conjunction with Chrysalis Books Group Plc.

International copyright reserved in all countries.
No part of this book may be reproduced in any form without written permission from the publisher.

Distributed in the United States by
Smart Apple Media
2140 Howard Drive West
North Mankato, Minnesota 56003

Library of Congress Control Number: 2004108782

ISBN 1-59389-206-3

Associate Publisher: Joyce Bentley
Project Editor: Debbie Foy
Editorial Assistant: Camilla Lloyd
Designer: Paul Cherrill
Illustrators: Ed Eaves, Jo Moore
and Molly Sage

Printed in China

10 9 8 7 6 5 4 3 2 1